P9-AGU-295

COED VOLLEYBALL
The Now Game

Virginia M. Nisle
Rio Hondo College

KENDALL/HUNT PUBLISHING COMPANY
2460 Kerper Boulevard, Dubuque, Iowa 52001

Copyright ©1977 by Kendall/Hunt Publishing Company

ISBN 0—8403—1795—6

All rights reserved. No part of this publication may be reproduced,
stored in a retrieval system, or transmitted, in any form or by any
means, electronic, mechanical, photocopying, recording, or otherwise,
without the prior written permission of the copyright owner.

Printed in the United States of America

401795 01

Preface to Readers

The game of coed volleyball has developed into a challenging and stimulating game that is suitable to all levels of competition. This game is now enjoyed in physical education classes, recreation leagues, interscholastic programs and by professional teams.

Coed Volleyball—The Now Game is a book written for students, instructors and recreation leaders who wish to learn or want to be updated on the current rules, skills and strategies of this popular game.

Chapter 1 covers a brief history of volleyball, basic rules, fouls and player line-up for the coed volleyball game.

Chapters 2 through 6 detail the fundamental skills of volleyball, such as overhead passing and setting, forearm passing, serving, spiking and blocking. Photographic descriptions, "up-to-date tips" and drills are included for each skill in these chapters. Student self-evaluation checklists are also included which will aid the serious students in improving their various ball-handling skills.

Chapter 7 is comprised of the intermediate skills of the underhand dig and overhead bump or dig.

Chapter 8 is devoted to offensive and defensive tactics. Strategy for the 4-2 system, switching, and covering positions behind the spike and block are shown in pictures and diagrams.

The *Terminology and Index* unit endeavors to clarify the many synonymous terms used in volleyball throughout the country. Page numbers of major reference are included with each term.

Acknowledgments

To the contributing photographers
  Louis Nunez, Whittier, CA.
  Don Kelsen, the cover photo, Whittier, CA.
To the players of the Rio Hondo College Coed Volleyball Team, and especially to their fine coach, Dan Smith.
To contributors of the artwork and diagrams
  Doug Hastings for his creative artwork
  Frances Horn for her excellent drawings
To the many who read, suggested, encouraged and inspired
  Ms. Virginia E. Young
  Dr. Hortense Hester
  Ms. Ruth Hunter
  Dr. Sharon Ratliffe

WITHDRAWN

774232

Contents

Chapter 1
AN OVERVIEW

Brief history. The game of volleyball originated in the United States in 1895, to meet the needs of "older" men who needed an indoor game that would not be too strenuous. It was invented by a YMCA Director from Holyoke, Massachusetts, William G. Morgan.

The "Y" has continued to be a staunch supporter of the game of volleyball throughout the years, but until the game was admitted to the Olympic Games in 1964, it did not receive the exposure and recognition it deserves. Currently, over 80 million people throughout the world participate in volleyball, and some authorities claim it to be the leading participation sport in the United States.

Very little written history can be found regarding the development of the coed volleyball game, although it is enjoyed both recreationally and competitively from the junior high school level up to and including the professional ranks.

Rules committees. Two major sets of rules have been used predominantly throughout the United States, those published by the United States Volleyball Association,[1] (USVBA), and those by the National Association for Girls and Women in Sport,[2] (NAGWS). In July, 1976, the USVBA Rules Committee recommended adoption of the rules of the game as authorized by the International Volleyball Federation, (IVF). NAGWS is also adopting the IVF rules and will print them according to their own format in their Fall, 1977, official rules guide. (IVF rules will be referred to throughout this book, as printed in the 1977 USVBA Rules previously cited.)

The court. Serving order. Playing positions. Rotation. The game of volleyball is played on a court 60 feet by 30 feet, with a net and a 2 inch line separating two teams of six players each. Figure 1.1 shows one-half of a court, with arrows indicating the direction of rotation upon receiving the ball for service. The $\bigcirc$ indicate the female players, $\triangle$ indicate the males.

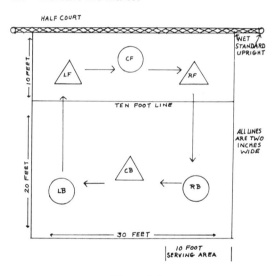

Figure 1.1

The first server shown in Figure 1.1 is a woman, (R.B., or right back) but a man could also be assigned this position. Second server, R.F., right forward; third server, C.F., center forward; fourth server, L.F.,

1. United States Volleyball Association, Official Rules, 1977, Guynes Printing Company, 615 North Stanton St., El Paso, Texas, 79901.

2. National Association for Girls and Women in Sport, Volleyball, 1977-1979. American Alliance for Health, Physical Education, and Recreation, 1201 Sixteenth Street, N.W., Washington, D.C., 20036

1

left forward; fifth server, L.B., left back; and sixth server, C.B., center back.

Coed Volleyball rules as authorized by the IVF:

> The rules in general shall govern play for females and males on the same team with the following exceptions: (a) Serving order and positions on the floor should be an alternation of male and female, or vice versa. (b) When the ball is played more than once by a team, one of these contacts must be by a female player. (c) The net height shall be 8 feet. (d) One back court player may also block when there is only one male player in the front line.

Beginning play. Before a game of volleyball begins, a coin is tossed to determine which team will serve the ball and which will receive the serve. Both teams must be in their correct playing positions when the ball is served, but may move to more advantageous positions after the ball is contacted. (Back row players may not spike in front of the 10 foot spiking line, however.)

To begin play, the R.B. player attempts to serve the ball from within the 10 foot serving area across the net and into the receiving team's court. Only 3 hits are allowed by a team in returning the ball to the opponent's court. (The first touch or hit on a block does not count as one of these hits; 3 more contacts are allowed after the block.)

After the ball is served, each team attempts to play the ball across the net and into the opponent's court so that it cannot be returned. The basic pattern of play is to pass the ball to the front row (setter) on the first hit, set the ball up for a spike on the second hit, and spike the ball forcibly down into the opponent's court on the third hit. This three-player-attack is also the basic attack strategy for the **power volleyball** game, which can be described as **playing the game with greater stress on skill, strategy and force** than is found in the former style of volleyball.

Scoring. If the served ball is not legally returned, a **point** is scored for the serving team. The same server continues serving as long as points are being scored. **Only** the serving team can score points. When they fail to score a point, side-out is declared and the ball is awarded to the opponent's, thus giving them the ball and the opportunity to serve and score points.

To win a game, a team must: (a) score 15 points and have a two point advantage (lead) over their opponents. (b) Play an eight minute game, leading their opponents by two or more points at the end of eight minutes of play. (**Timed games should be used only** when strict adherence of a time schedule would make 15 point games impractical.) In case of a tie game, or a lead of only one point, play continues until one team gains a two point advantage.

A match consists of winning three games from one's opponent. (In case of limited time schedules or when a team must play several matches in a day, two games won would determine the winner.)

Teams change ends of the court after each game, and in the middle of the **deciding** game, the third or fifth, depending on whether the winner is determined by winning two or three games. (The middle of a 15 point game is the eight point mark, or four minutes in an eight point game.)

Fouls That Frequently Occur in Coed Play

1. Illegal serves—ball is served from outside serving area, is served into the net or out-of-bounds, is hit from the server's holding hand.
2. Players on serving or receiving team are out of rotation order or **overlapping** at the time the ball is contacted.
3. Ball is sent over the net with no contact by a woman when more than one hit has occurred on that side.
4. Player attempts to receive or play spiked ball with an overhand pass rather than the forearm pass.

5. Back-row player comes to the net to block when there are already two men in the front row.
6. Back-row player spikes from in front of the 10 foot spiking line.
7. Blocker reaches over the net and contacts ball before it is being returned to his side.
8. Player touches net during play or continuation of play.
9. Player goes over the centerline before ball is dead. (Play is legal if some part of offending foot or feet remains in contact with the centerline.)
10. Player makes a double-hit on a play.
11. Player throws, pushes or lifts ball on an attempted play.
12. More than 3 hits occur in playing the ball over the net. (The block does not count as one of the 3 allowed hits.)
13. Player or team delays the game.
14. Player displays unsportsmanlike conduct, such as stamping the feet or yelling at an opponent who is attempting to play the ball.

Chapter 2
THE OVERHAND PASS AND SET

Most of the "tips" that follow may be applied equally to both overhand passing and setting, as both skills require the same basic body mechanics. **Passing** is the movement of the ball from one teammate to another, while setting is a more precise method which is used to set the ball up near the net at a height advantageous for the hitter to spike the ball.

Ready position for overhand pass and set. Players must learn to anticipate a developing play and respond to it as required. The body may need to be high, medium or low, depending on the height of the ball being received and the distance and height of the **intended** pass or set. See Figure 2.1 and "tips."

In moving to the ball, player maintains a fairly low body position and does quick slide steps or skips in getting **to** the ball and positioning body **beneath** it for the pass. It is imperative to keep eyes on the ball for good passing and setting!

Contact of the ball, correct hand positions. Players should make contact with the ball about 5 or 6 inches off the forehead. It is important to watch the ball through the "window" formed by the thumbs and fingers, and let it come to you rather than to reach out for it. See Figure 2.2 and hand position tips.

Follow-through. Players frequently overlook the importance of a complete

Figure 2.0

follow-through for achieving the necessary height and distance for the desired pass or set. See Figure 2.3 and also the "tips."

An ideal pass for a setter to handle is one that would land on top of the forehead if missed. The arc of this **pass** would be 5 to 6 feet higher than the setter's head.

The desired height of a **set** depends on the jumping ability of the spiker being set, the opponents' block and defense, and the intended **play** by the offense. A normal set is one that loops in a high arc and drops 1 or 2 feet from the net at the left or right forward position.

Back set. The back set is a technique used to deceive blockers who are preparing to block the spiker that the setter is facing. It is also used when the pass to the setter is too high to be cleanly front set. (See Figure 2.4.)

Figure 2.1

Ready position "tips".

1. Move quickly for the ball, keep weight on balls of feet, one foot ahead of other, both feet pointing in direction of the pass.
2. Place hands in ready position, wrists back, elbows at shoulder level.
3. Keep knees flexed and ready to lower or elevate the body, as needed.

Figure 2.2

Hand position, contact "tips".

1. Place hands in triangle, thumbs about 2 inches apart.
2. Cock the wrists, thumbs toward the face, keep them relaxed until contact.
3. Just before contact, start extending legs and shifting weight in direction of the pass.
4. Upon contact, extend arms, fingers and wrists vigorously upward in line with intended flight of the ball. The hands finish as though pushing open a set of swinging doors.

Figure 2.3

Follow-through "tips".

1. Extend arms, wrists and fingers **equally** to ensure accuracy.
2. Extend legs and body **totally** and in an upward line with the play to get the needed power for higher sets and longer passes.

Figure 2.4

6

The back set is executed much like the front set (over-hand set) except that the setter takes a position directly under the ball, the hands are laid backward with palms upward, the shoulders rotate slightly upward and backward, and the back is arched upon contact with the ball. (Setters should be careful not to arch the back too soon, thus alerting the blockers to the play.) See Figure 2.5.

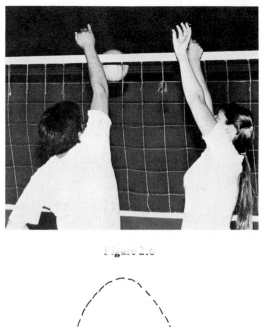

Figure 2.6

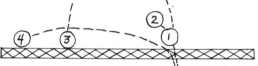

Figure 2.5

On the follow-through, the head should be kept up; the arm and hands also extending up and back.

Play sets. As setters become confident in their setting ability, they should attempt to use strategy in their sets. They should evaluate their opponents' strengths and weaknesses and deliver a variety of sets for their spikers, or **play sets.** Low, vertical sets are being practiced by the players in Figure 2.6. The setter may stand on a chair and hold the ball for the spiker to hit with a quick, short armswing and wrist snap. Next, the setter may toss the ball a foot or two above the net for the spiker to hit. This prepares setters and hitters for the sets indicated in Figure 2.7.

One-set, or Jap set. Ball is set just 6 to 12 inches above the net. Spiker must jump just prior to the setter's contact of the ball.

Two-set. This set is just 2 to 3 feet above the net, so spiker must jump right after the setter contacts the ball.

Three-set. This set is of normal height, but is placed between the left forward and center forward positions. (Or between the end and middle blockers.)

Four-set, or shoot set. This set travels low and fast toward the sideline, about 2 feet above the net.

Figure 2.7

Purpose of play sets:
1. Beat the block—They go up late.
2. Split the block—Hit between blockers.
3. Freeze the block—To get one-on-one situation.

Additional play sets may be used by many advanced players, and some may not agree with the numbers as assigned above. (Some may use a three-shoot set and four normal set, etc.) The important point is for setters and spikers to coordinate their plays and call them out as they practice them. **Play sets are called off if the pass is poor.** Figures 2.8-2.10.

Figure 2.10

Setter makes good set of a low pass.

Figure 2.8

Setter elects to "punch" this high pass over the net to opponent's side.

Figure 2.9

Setter "tips" high pass to opponent's side.

Drills for Passing and Setting

Accurate setting and passing is essential before any attack can occur, therefore, much practice time must be devoted to learning and improving these skills. (To many students, volleyball *is* passing and setting. For this reason, these skills are frequently selected as the first to be taught.)

The following drills proceed from the beginning basic hand position on the ball to challenging, competitive drills which involve considerable player movement.

Students should check the "Goof Check List" at the end of the chapter to periodically evaluate their progress.

KEY TO DRILL FORMATIONS

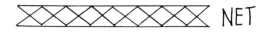 NET

 PATH OF BALL

—————————→ PATH OF PLAYER

Figure 2.11

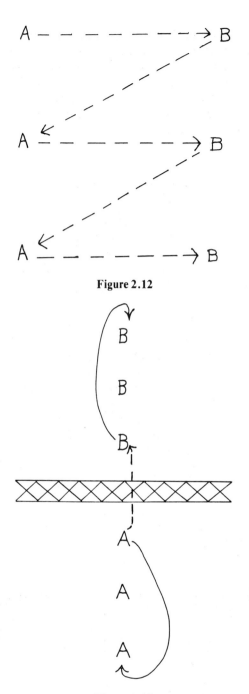

Figure 2.12

Figure 2.13

Stress passing the ball one-half step in front of teammate so that he can step into the ball, meeting it above and in front of the face.

Drill 1

Squads are divided into two lines, *A* and *B,* as shown in Figure 2.12. The first player in line *A* kneels down, puts ball on floor, places hands in triangle on ball, and then stands, facing line *B*. From a forward stride stand, a looping chest pass is made to line *B*.

Drill 2

Squads are divided, 3 players on each side of the net. First player in line A passes the ball over the net to first player in line B, then goes to end of own line, etc. This drill should help players achieve better height and control of their passes. See Figure 2.13.

Drill 3

Each squad forms a circle with a leader in the center. The leader passes the ball 10 to 12 feet high and one-half step in front of player B, who attempts to return a high, controlled pass to the leader. Practice continues around the circle; the leader must always

move under the return pass, **set the feet** and **be turned** toward the next player as he makes his pass. See Figure 2.14.

Figure 2.14

Drill 4

Players in Circle. (Figure 2.15.) In this drill, all players follow the pattern of the leader in the previous drill. Player A passes to B. *While the ball is in the air,* B turns, sets feet, then passes to C, etc. The key to this drill is getting the player to give high, accurate passes to the next in line. (This drill should be repeated in both directions.)

Drill 5

Players lined up one behind the other, facing the wall. Each player has 10 practice passes against the wall. Then the squad members each do a pass, go to the end of the line, etc., trying to build up as many completed passes as they can until someone misses. (This drill is good for competition between squads, or for a squad to improve

its own record from week to week.) Figure 2.16.

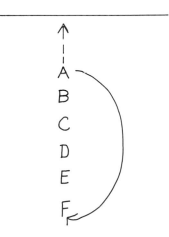

Figure 2.15

Figure 2.16

Drill 6

Players form a triangle, 2 or 3 at each point position. First player in line A passes to first player in line B, then immediately follows pass, going to the *end* of line B. First player in line B passes to first player in line C, then goes to the end of line C, etc. (This drill creates lots of player movement and encourages players to think and anticipate.) See Figure 2.17.

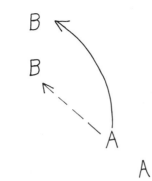

Figure 2.17

Drill 7

Squad in semicircle facing the leader. To teach players to get under low passes for proper setting, leader *bounces* ball to each at chin or neck level, thus forcing a lower crouch position to correctly position body under the ball for a good set. See Figure 2.18.

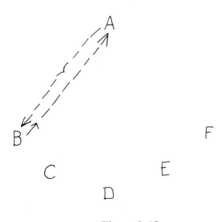

Figure 2.18

Drill 8

Two lines facing each other 10 feet apart, with a leader in the center. The leader in the center makes only **short** passes, while lines B and C alternate a short pass to the center with a long pass to the opposite line. (On long pass to opposite line, leader must turn quickly to be ready for short pass from the new direction.) See Figure 2.19.

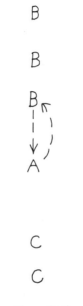

Figure 2.19

Drill 9

Squad lines up in 3 stations around basketball key, as shown in Figure 2.20. First player in line A passes ball to Player in line B, who attempts to "set" ball into the basket. Players in line C are "retrievers," returning ball to line A. Each player may be given 3, 5, or 10 attempts at setting, with 2 points being recorded for a basket, and 1 point if the ball touches the rim.

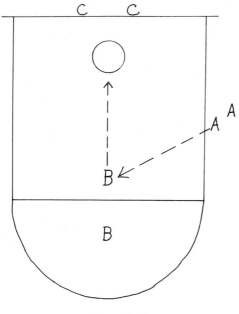

Figure 2.20

Drill 10

Before attempting the following back set drills, each player should practice doing high overhead volleys to *self,* first attempting to stay in small area, later on adding a 1/2 turn between each set, etc.

In Figure 2.21, *A* sets ball high to self, turns under ball and back sets player in line *B,* then moves to end of own line.

Figure 2.21

Drill 11

Player A gives a short pass to player B, who then back sets player C, who then gives a long pass to A, etc. Other players should move into the drill after 5 or so successful back sets. See Figure 2.22.

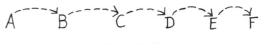

Figure 2.22

Drill 12

Players are lined up as in Figure 2.23, one behind the other, and all facing forward. Each player does a back set until ball reaches player F. Player F does a high pass to self, turns and starts the back set drill in opposite direction.

Figure 2.23

Drill 13

Player A passes to the wall, player B gets under the rebound and back sets A, etc.

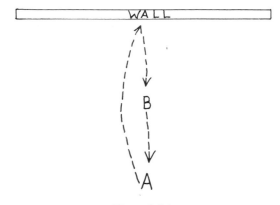

Figure 2.24

Practice Game-Pass and Set

1. The game is started by giving a pass (free ball) to opponents.
2. The player receiving the ball should call for it, move under it and pass it to the setter, or C.F.
3. The third contact should be a long pass, deep into opponents' court.
4. Only legal passes are allowed, no spikes!
5. Three hits should be encouraged and may be required.
6. A girl must hit the ball if more than one hit occurs on a side.
7. Players should call own "net" fouls, obvious illegal hits and any "touch" when ball goes out of bounds.
8. The "server" should call out the score before putting the ball in play, giving own team's score first.
9. Teams rotate as in official game.

Student Evaluation or *Goof* List for Passing and Setting

(Check appropriate column)

	Often	Sometimes	Seldom
1. Am I slow in reacting to the play and getting **ready**?			
2. Do I forget to turn and face the direction of my pass or set?			
3. Am I unsure as to when it is my play?			
4. Are my knees too straight or stiff for doing long passes?			
5. Do I let my elbows droop below shoulder level?			
6. Do I fail to form a triangle with my thumbs and fingers?			
7. Are my wrists **stiff** rather than cocked for action?			
8. Do I **reach** out for the ball rather than letting it come to me?			
9. Do I **slap** the ball, creating noisy hits?			
10. Do I **quit** after contacting the ball rather than having a strong follow-through?			

Chapter 3
THE FOREARM PASS

The forearm pass is sometimes referred to as the bump, scoop, underhand pass, forearm bounce and two-hand dig. It is referred to by some authorities as **the** pass, as it is used almost exclusively for receiving serves and controlling opponents' spikes. It is also used for net recovery and for playing any ball approaching a player below waist level.

Figure 3.0

The forearm pass increases the time a player has to get ready for a play, and also increases the range he may cover. Figure 3.1 shows a player in excellent form for receiving the serve.

Ready position for the Forearm pass. If there is any secret to good passing, it is to plan ahead! Players should familiarize themselves with the "tips" for the ready position before determining which hand position to select.

Hand positions for the forearm pass. Figure 3.2 shows four popular hand positions for the forearm pass. Players and instructors should study the merits of each and

Figure 3.1

Ready position "tips".
1. Take a semi-crouch stance with weight on balls of the feet, shoulder width apart.
2. Arms should be loose and relaxed, hands out for balance.
3. Player should watch the serve carefully, line up with it and get the body under it for the pass.

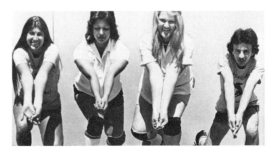

Figure 3.2

then select the style that works best for each individual.

Thumb over palm. The thumb of the bottom hand is placed across the fingers of the top hand, as shown by the player on the left.

The second player is demonstrating the **clenched fist** method. One hand forms a clenched fist and the other hand wraps snugly around it, the thumbs are parallel. This is perhaps the most popular method as it allows almost out-of-reach balls to be hit legally with the hands. (Ball hit by hands in the thumb over palm method would most likely result in a foul being called.)

The third player is demonstrating the **curled fingers method.** The hands are slightly cupped, one hand in the other, thumbs parallel. This creates a flat rebounding surface. This method is most popular with competitive teams.

The fourth method is the clapped hands position. The hands are placed together, as though clapping hands. Some players slightly clasp the tips of the fingers to prevent the hands from separating before completing the pass. (This method was frequently seen being used by players in the recent Olympic Games.)

Contacting the ball. Upon selecting the hand position to be used for the forearm pass, the player is now ready to "put it all together."

"Tips" for contacting the pass.
1. The back is fairly straight and the buttocks **low** upon contacting the ball.
2. The arms are away from the body; the elbows are kept straight to make a firm rebound surface for the ball.
3. The ball is contacted simultaneously on both forearms, 5 or 6 inches above the hands.
4. Upon contact, there is a slight forward shift of weight, extension of legs and a shrug of the shoulders.
5. The wrists are rolled forward and downward, an important "tip" for those who allow the ball to roll up the arms or who sometimes hit it behind themselves.

Follow-through. The player continues the extension of legs; the arms move upward to about shoulder level. The player should not think of this upward motion as a swing, but merely the finish of the pass. Most swing passes result in uncontrolled play with the ball going out of bounds.

Net recovery. The player in Figure 3.4 is making an excellent "save" of a pass into

Figure 3.4

If this play is to be the third hit, player must finish the pass by dipping the left shoulder, cradling the ball in the forearms, and by using body rotation and arm movement up in the direction of the intended pass.

Figure 3.3

16

the net. She has taken a wide stride for balance, is well below the ball for the rebound and is watching the ball intently. To convert the play to a set for a spike, she must keep the shoulders parallel throughout the pass.

Figure 3.5 shows player picking up a hard-driven spike by absorbing much of the force with his body. This impact often drives the player to a "seat" as he follows through after the pass. (See Chapter 7 for half-roll.)

Figure 3.5

Drill 1.

Squad in semicircle, each in "ready position" facing a leader. Ball is thrown to each player in turn, who returns ball with controlled forearm pass to the leader. Ball should be thrown progressively harder, as players learn to move to the ball and adjust to throws of various heights. Random throws should also be used to keep the players "on their toes." (As skill of players increases, leaders should use spiking rather than throwing the ball.) See Figure 3.6.

Drill 2

Squad in circle, each player about 6 feet apart. Ball is thrown to first player who may then use a forearm pass to anyone in the circle. Ball continues with forearm passes to anyone in circle, but each player must call for his/her hit. Squads may compete for the most number of passes before an error occurs. Figure 3.7.

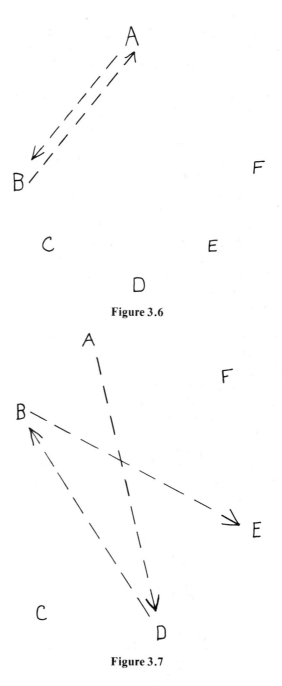

Figure 3.6

Figure 3.7

Drill 3

Squad is divided, 3 on each side of the net. Each player combines an overhand set to *self* followed by a forearm pass across the

17

net to a teammate. (By combining the two skills before passing the ball, each player immediately has an accurate picture of his/her command of the first two skills taught.) Although the first attempts of this drill may be discouraging, later practices should show much improvement in control and quickness in getting to the ball. Player goes to end of own line after completing his/her turn. See Figure 3.8.

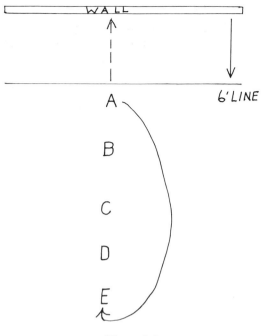

Figure 3.9

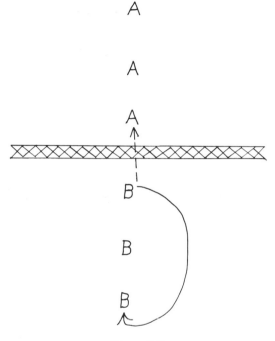

Figure 3.8

Drill 4

Squad lines up facing wall, leader is behind a 6 foot restraining line. He tosses ball underhand to wall and then attempts to do 5 continuous forearm passes. After each player has practiced 5 passes, the squad does continuous passing (3, 2, or 1 hit each, then going to the end of the line). See Figure 3.9.

Drill 5

Players form a triangle, 2 or 3 at each position. First player in line A tosses ball to first player in line B for a forearm pass to

Line C, etc. Player follows pass, moving to end of line passed to. Forearm passes should be stressed, but overhand passes may be used for higher passes. See Figure 3.10.

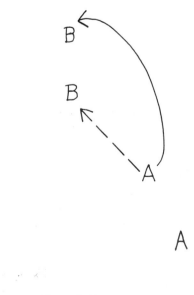

Figure 3.10

Drill 6

Two squads combined, 3 players at each line as indicated in Figure 3.11. First player in line A gives a forearm pass to the line B, then goes to end of line B. Line B passes to Line C, Line C to D, and then back to line A. (Player always goes to end of line to which he passed the ball.)

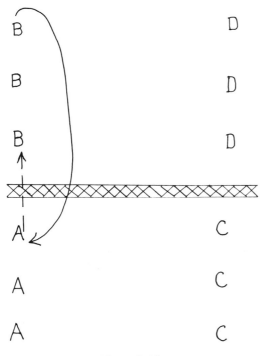

Figure 3.11

Drill 7

Combination serve and receive drill. One squad lined up to practice underhand serves, other team in receiving formation. See Figure 3.12. Each server attempts 5 serves. Receiving team must use a forearm pass to setter (the C.F.) who then "sets" the L.F. or R.F. player. This player catches the ball and rolls it back to serving line. After 5 serves, new server takes turn and the receiving team rotates so that all can practice each position. (In later practices, overhand serves may be used and switching of setter and hitter to ac-commodate better offense.) Service reception is the most difficult part of the game for many beginning players; therefore, ample time must be accorded to it. To make the practice challenging, the serving team may be awarded a point each time its serve is not legally played; the receiving team would win a point each time it successfully passes to the setter, who sets the left or right forward. The forward then rolls the ball back to opponents. (A student referee may be used to start play and call out points and fouls.)

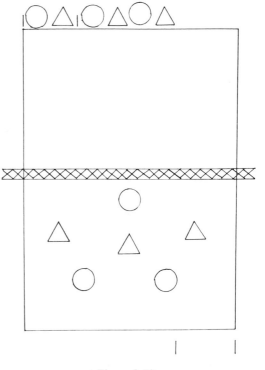

Figure 3.12

Drill 8

Squad lined up facing wall. Leader tosses ball underhand for player to "save" with a forearm bounce pass back to the leader. See Figure 3.13.

Drill 9

Squad lined up facing net. Leader tosses ball underhand into center of net for player

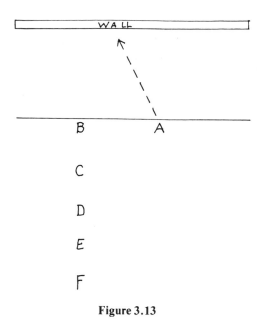

Figure 3.13

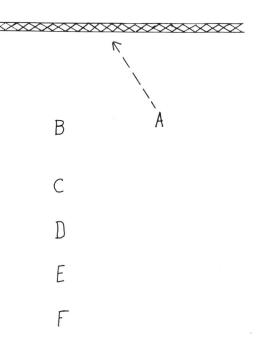

Figure 3.14

to *drop* and save. If net is loose, a player may be used to secure it at the bottom so that players may have a successful experience in learning net recovery. (They may also start drill with side to the net and in a low ready position to play the ball.) As they progress, ball may be thrown overhand at upper portion of net. This should be demonstrated at any rate, so that players may become aware of the different rebound plays at the net. See Figure 3.14.

Practice Game—Forearm Pass, Set and Directed Pass

1. The game is started by passing a free ball to opponents court, or an underhand serve may be used.

2. The player receiving the ball should call for the ball and use a **forearm pass** to the C.F.

3. The third hit should be a precise pass to a "hole" or weak area in opponents' court. No spikes!

4. Three hits are **required** by each side in this game, and all rules listed in the Chapter 2 Practice Game apply.

5. Stress calling for the ball, knowing each person's territory and not encroaching on it, only legal hits allowed for "point" or "side-out" and verbal tips and cues should be encouraged. (Mine-out—GIRL-etc.)

Self-Evaluation or *Goof* List for the
Forearm Pass

(Check appropriate column)

	Often	Sometimes	Seldom
1. Am I slow in lining up with the ball and planting my feet?			
2. Do I lean forward rather than get low for the pass?			
3. Am I unsure of my hand position on contact with ball?			
4. Do I contact the ball on hands and wrists rather than on the forearms?			
5. Do I bend my elbows, sending the ball up or behind me?			
6. Do I swing at the ball, creating wild hits?			
7. Do I forget to shrug my shoulders and roll my wrists on the follow-through?			
8. Do I run with hands together, reaching out for the ball?			
9. Do I forget to drop quickly for recovery plays out of the net?			
10. Do I use a small stance instead of a balanced stride position, one foot forward in playing the pass?			

Chapter 4
THE SERVE

Since a team may only score points when it has the serve, (or service) this is a vital skill to practice and perfect. A player should develop a style of serving that is consistent, accurate and difficult for opponents to return.

Figure 4.0

The underhand serve. This serve is considered the easiest to learn and control and, therefore, most likely to give success to those just learning the game.

Hand positions for serving. Figure 4.1 shows 3 hand positions for contacting the serve. The fist position (player on the right) will afford the greatest power for the serve: the ball is contacted by the heel of the hand and the knuckles.

Directions for right-handed player: Stand facing the net, left foot ahead of right, knees relaxed and body leaning slightly forward. Hold the ball in the left hand with that arm extending across the body and in line with the hitting (right) hand. With weight on back foot, take a long backswing with the

Figure 4.1

Hand positions for serving.
(Left) Open hand.
(Center) Cupped Hand.
(Right) Fist.

Rules for serving.
1. Server must serve from within the serving area.
2. Server may not step on or over serving line (endline) until ball is contacted.
3. The ball must be thrown or released before it is hit.
4. The serve cannot be made with two hands.
5. The serve must be hit, not thrown or pushed.
6. Ball must not touch the net on way to opponents' court.
7. Server must be player in the R.B. position.
8. All teammates must be in correct playing positions when the serve is contacted.

right hand. Release the ball just prior to the heel of the right hand making contact with the ball. See Figure 4.2.

23

Figure 4.2

Follow-through. Accuracy in this serve requires a precise follow-through in the direction of the intended serve. Player should keep eyes on the ball throughout the serve to ensure a solid, smooth and coordinated serve. See Figure 4.3.

Figure 4.3

Sidearm serve. This serve proceeds much as the underhand serve except the servers feet are now pointing toward the sideline. (The left foot **should** be slightly ahead of the right.) The ball is held in left hand with the fingers pointing toward the sideline. The

right arm swings back at shoulder level and parallel to floor or court surface. See Figure 4.4. This server is much more difficult for receivers to handle due to its greater speed, spinning or floating action and its angle of entry into opponents' court.

Figure 4.4

Overhand Serves. The majority of leading players use an overhand serve, but there are many styles from which to choose. Each player should select the serve in which he can become most proficient.

Overhand floater or "punch" serve. This serve is relatively easy to learn, yet difficult for the opposition to handle. The player stands facing the net, left foot ahead of right. The ball is held at chin level and in line with the striking hand. The ball is thrown about 3 feet above the head. The server cocks arm, steps forward and contacts ball an inch or two below its center using the heel of the hand. The wrist remains stiff after contact and there is as little follow-through as possible. See Figure 4.5.

Topspin Serve. This serve has a fast dropping action that is difficult for inexperienced players to receive, but it is not as deceptive as the floater. The preparation and timing is similar, except that the ball is tossed a foot higher and the arm whips into the hit in a spiking action. See Figure 4.6.

id="1"

Figure 4.5

Various effects of the floater serve.

1. With valve stem pointed down upon contact, ball drops rapidly after crossing net.
2. With valve up, ball goes deeper into opponents' court.
3. With valve placed to one side, ball should break to that side.
4. With valve toward opponents, ball should wobble from side to side.

Figure 4.6

Contact for topspin serve.

1. Heel of hand contacts ball at its exact center.
2. A vigorous wrist snap imparts topspin to the serve.
3. On the follow-through the arm continues to swing forward in line with the serve.

The roundhouse serve. This serve is used by National and World championship teams, but is mastered by relatively few players. It is, therefore, very difficult to receive, and is the most effective serve of all.

The server stands with left shoulder toward the net, feet shoulder-width apart. The ball is tossed 3-5 feet overhead. See Figure 4.7. As ths ball is tossed with the left hand, the right hand drops to the side, the knees bend, and the body leans slightly backward. See Figure 4.8. With a cupped

Figure 4.7

Figure 4.8

right hand, the arm whips up to meet the ball in a windmill fashion. See Figure 4.9. For a floater, just the heel of the hand makes contact with the ball. See Figure 4.9.

Figure 4.9

Serving Strategy. As players become confident in their serving skills, they will want to use this offensive weapon to win outright points (aces) for their teams. To better accomplish this, they must learn to read the opponents' formations to spot strengths and weaknesses. (Do they have weak passers? Does one player play out of position to "cover" for another? Is the front row back too far or up too close? Is the setter slow in getting into position when serves go deep to the corners? Is one spiker particularly weak?)

"To be precise with the serve is better than to hit the serve hard."[1] McGown lists the following situations to *never miss* your serve:

"1. After a time out
2. After a substitution
3. After a teammate has missed
4. When the game is close at the end
5. The first serve of a game
6. After opponents have run several points"

One more serving premise: A team must serve more aces than serving errors.

Serving Drills

The following drills may be used to learn and practice both the underhand and overhand serves. Rules relating to proper serving should be emphasized throughout the practice. A referee or leader may be used to start each serve, signal fouls and check for the readiness of receiving players. *Concentration* on every serve is essential for achieving accuracy and precision!

Drill 1

Two squads lined up behind serving lines, each squad lined up as in Figure 4.10. "A" will serve a prescribed number of serves and then go to the end of the line to assist in retrieving opponents' serves, passing them to the new server. Targets, such as towels, may be added for teams to practice hitting with each serve. Competition between teams for best scores on serving should stimulate greater efforts and results. See Figure 4.10.

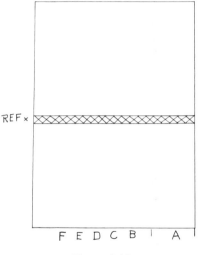

Figure 4.10

Drill 2

One squad is lined up for serving practice as in Drill 1. The second squad is positioned

1. McGown, Carl, information taken from mimeographed material used with physical education classes and teams.

on the court for receiving practice, as in Figure 4.5. As the serving team changes servers, receiving team should rotate so that everyone may have practice receiving in each position.

Drill 3

Players having particular serving problems may be assisted with extra practice by utilizing the areas between courts or at the side of a court. Weaker players may start in front of the serving line, gradually working their way back to the official distance of 30 feet. See Figure 4.11.

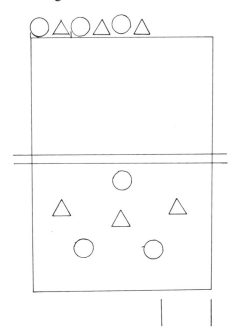

Figure 4.11

Drill 4

To learn new serving styles or techniques, the wall may be used for extra practice stations, allowing many more serves to be practiced in a limited amount of time. See Figure 4.12.

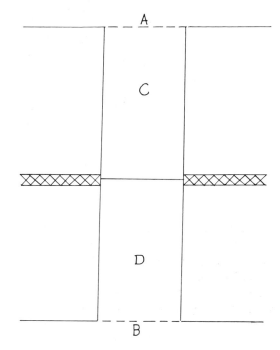

Figure 4.12

Drill 5

Serving targets (or towels) are set up as in Figure 4.13. Two serves are allowed to each numbered area, and two points are awarded for each hit. One point is awarded if serve is legal, but missed correct target.

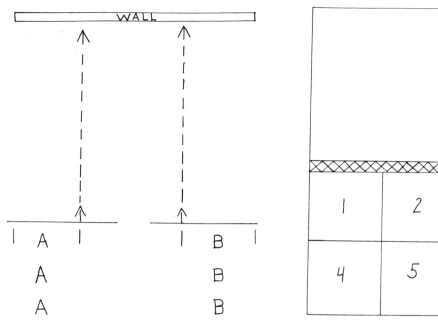

| Figure 4.13 | Figure 4.14 |

Student Evaluation or *Goof* List for Serving

(Check appropriate column)

	Often	Sometimes	Seldom
1. Do I set up for my serve with consistent stance and position?			
2. Do I concentrate on the exact spot to contact the ball every time?			
3. Is my toss and swing correct for my style of serve?			
4. Is my hit solid and powerful?			
5. Can I serve accurately to target areas?			
6. Do my serves usually clear the net?			
7. Can I effectively serve more than one style or method?			
8. Can I read the opponents' weaknesses and strengths and serve accordingly?			
9. Do I move into the court quickly after my serve to be ready for the next play?			
10. Do I avoid footfaults and other service errors?			

Chapter 5
THE SPIKE

The spike is a hard driven ball into the opponents' court. It is usually a team's third contact of the ball, being preceded by the pass and set. It has often been described as the most difficult act to master in any sport. It requires excellent timing of the jump, a proper armswing, and a solid contact with a moving ball which is directed to a specific area. It is the basic weapon of attack, often psychologically overpowering teams lacking in spiking skill.

The approach for the spike. Figure 5.0 shows the spiker as he gathers speed and momentum. He is utilizing full armswings as he prepares for his jump or take-off.

Figure 5.0

Spike approach tips.
1. Start approach 10-12 feet from the net.
2. After 3 or 4 steps, the spiker **plants** weight on the heels, arms are back and body is in a semi-crouch position.
3. The last step of the approach is longer than the others, aiding the spiker in the **plant** which helps convert the forward momentum into the upward jump.

Figure 5.1 shows the path and steps in the approach and the plant for the jump. For right-handed spikers, this on-hand hitting position is easier and more powerful from the left forward position.

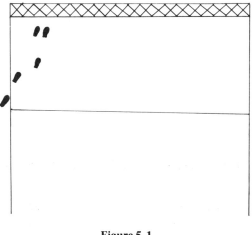

Figure 5.1

The jump and armswing. The jump should be from both feet, about 2 to 3 feet from where the spiker expects to contact the ball. His weight transfers (rocks) from the heels to the balls of the feet as he swings his arms vigorously to achieve a maximum jump. At this point the ankles and legs extend explosively.

The left hand may point toward the set, while the right arm is cocked with the right shoulder rotated back as far as possible. See Figure 5.2.

Contact and follow-through. The right elbow leads in initiating the spike, with the simultaneous drive of the left arm and shoulder. See Figure 5.3. The knees also begin to straighten and the body kips for-

Figure 5.2

Added power may be gained by arching the back and slightly bending the knees. The entire approach and jump should be smooth and "quiet."

Figure 5.3

ward. This action forces the shoulders to rotate until parallel with the net. The right arm continues to straighten to a full reach. The ball is contacted 6-12 inches in front of the right shoulder by the heel of the cupped hand, followed immediately by a vigorous snap of wrist and fingers over the top of the ball.

After the contact, the right arm swings across the body to avoid striking the net. The play must land in a controlled balanced posi-

tion, knees slightly bent to prevent falling over the centerline or causing injury.

Spiking angles. The beginning spiker may be satisfied to merely drive a hard spike ver the net without any concern for placement. As he gains confidence in his spiking skill, however, he will wish to be able to hit the ball to the area called for by the game situation. To accomplish this, the spiker should approach the ball squarely with the shoulders parallel to the net, as in Figure 5.4. He may then hit the various spiking angles shown in Figure 5.5. All spikes should be practiced from both sides of the court, and later on from the center position, also.

Figure 5.4

Spiker is arching back and bending the knees for added power on his spike.

Spiking variations. When the defense is "dug in" expecting a hard spike, the best hit may be one of reduced speed, and placed to a hole or weak area in the opponents' defense.

Change-of-pace (soft) spikes. The spiker should start as with his hard spikes until his hand starts forward to hit the ball. The speed of the swing is then reduced to half-speed and the ball is contacted a little below center with considerable topspin. The ball will thus clear the blockers and drop into the court.

Figure 5.6 shows the areas that may be vulnerable to this shot. Some players are adept at spotting these holes and calling them out to the hitter.

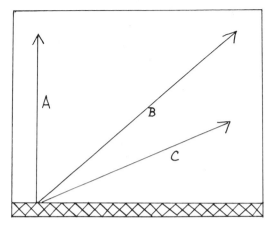

Figure 5.5

A. Down-the-line spike. From the on-hand side, the spiker swings straight through the ball to hit it as shown.
B. Power-angle spike. This is the most popular hit with beginning and intermediate spikers, and therefore, the first angle blockers will attempt to block.
C. Cross-court spike. This spike is more difficult to do from the on-hand side. The spiker proceeds as in the other spikes, but as the hand begins the backswing, the trunk is rotated from the hips, thus allowing the head and spiking hand to line up behind the ball.

The Dink. The spiker should again proceed as in the power spike until both arms swing up to shoulder level. The spiking hand then reaches up for the ball with elbows, wrist and fingers extended. There is no wrist snap or follow-through, just a soft tap over the block. See Figure 5.7.

Figure 5.8 shows an experienced spiker disguising his spike and executing a good **cut shot** while the blocker is obviously attempting to block the power angle spike.

Quick offense. The Japanese Men's and Women's National teams brought a new and

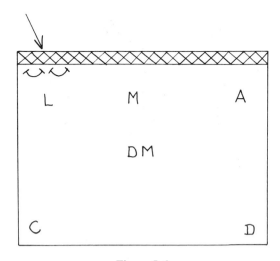

Figure 5.6

Key for diagram:
L. Line behind blockers.
M. Middle front.
A. Sharp angle near net.
DM. Deep middle.
C&D. Corners.

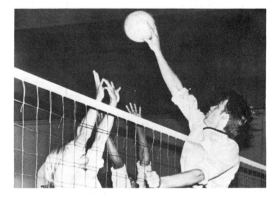

Figure 5.7

Figure 5.8

exciting dimension to the game of volleyball when they introduced the **quick offense.** Players should review the play sets described in Figures 2.6 and 2.7 in Chapter 2. The main emphasis to be remembered is that of **quickness** in hitting **down** rather than in power and full armswing.

Spiking Drills and Warm-Ups

Both spiking and blocking require sudden and explosive action from muscles of the legs, back, shoulders, arms and wrists. Many warm-ups and drills should be used, therefore, to prevent injury as well as to increase the jumping skills of the players.

1. Players should jog around courts, jumping to touch the basketball nets or some type of **challenge.** Use two-step jump.
2. Practice Sargeant Jump along wall space. Chalk may be used for marking, or yardsticks taped up with **standing stretch** and jumping **reach** measured.
3. Players line up along the net opposite opponent of approximately the same height. On signal, they jump and try to touch hands over the net.
4. In open order formation, players practice a jump and do 1/4 turn, landing in a 12 inch square. Repeat with 1/2 turn, and in both directions. Emphasize good use of arms to assist in the turn and control.
5. Practice the **approach** from open order formation before moving onto the courts. Emphasize steps, armswing, jump, swing and the landing.

Drill 1

Two lines of players facing each other. Player A holds ball **high** in left hand and in front of the right shoulder. With a cupped hand, A reaches and hits ball out of hand, snapping it downward into a bounce to player B. Player in line repeats, etc. Figure 5.9.

Figure 5.9

Drill 2

Squad lines up facing the wall, as in Figure 5.10. Each has turn spiking the ball to the floor and then the wall, and tries to "keep it going." The spiking should start from 10-15 feet, gradually working farther back.

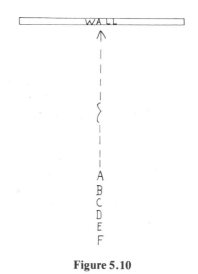

Figure 5.10

32

Drill 3

Squad is lined up facing net, as in Figure 5.11. Each practices the approach to the net, jump, reach, and then a controlled take-off and landing. Next the leader may give a toss for the spiker to hit over the net. Next the leader sets the spiker, attempting to set the ball 4-5 feet higher than the net and 12-18 inches from the net.

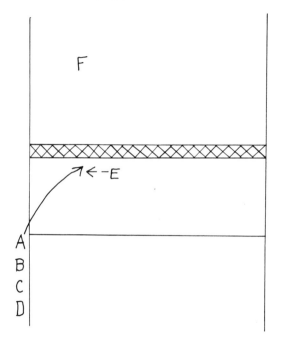

Figure 5.11

Finally, the spiker starts the drill by passing the ball to the setter, moves to the net as the setter sets the ball up for the spike.

Drill 4

Figure 5.12 shows a three station combination drill sometimes called Russian Pepper. Player A spikes the ball to player B who gives a forearm pass to C, who sets A. Play should again be practiced in both directions, then players change duties.

Drill 5

As players achieve skill and control in spiking, they are ready for the **stand-by** for

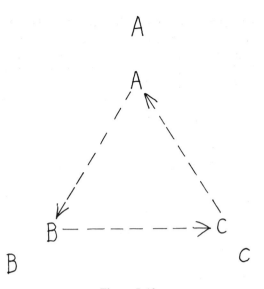

Figure 5.12

spiking warm-up, Pepper. Figure 5.13 shows A spiking to D, as other players wait their turns and retrieve "wild" hits. Spikers should concentrate on making their jump 2-3 feet in front of a spot where they expect to contact the ball.

Players should rotate every 5 hits or so, and all drills should be practiced from both left and right side of the court.

Figure 5.13

Student Evaluation or *Goof* List for Spiking

	Often	Sometimes	Seldom
	(Check appropriate column)		

1. Do I time my approach so that it is not too late or too early?
2. Do I use a two-step jump and good use of arms for added height?
3. Do I crouch low, using a rocking from heels to balls of feet and good leg extension?
4. Do I keep myself behind the ball for powerful angle shots?
5. Do I check my momentum, landing in a controlled, balanced position?
6. Do I use a cupped hand rather than fist?
7. When I get a poor set, do I adjust my hit, rather than "whaling away?"
8. Do I try to use change-of-pace shots, always attempting to keep every hit in bounds?
9. Do I practice line and cross-courts?
10. Do I practice dinks, with a good reach, but no breaking of the wrist?

Chapter 6
THE BLOCK

As teams learn the power attack play of the pass, set and spike, they must also be introduced to defensive tactics to counteract the power attack.

The block is the first line of defense, and also the best. This skill is accomplished by jumping into the air close to the net, arms and hands extended, making contact with the ball just after it has been hit.

Figure 6.0

Tasks of the blocker.
1. To prevent the spike from coming to their side of the net.
2. To slow down the ball and make it playable by a teammate.
3. To force the spiker into an error by upsetting his timing or causing him to change his choice of spike.

Ready position tips.
1. Arms up and ready.
2. Body in semi-crouch, feet parallel to net and shoulder width apart.
3. Eyes on setter, ball and the spiker.

One blocker. When playing against inexperienced spikers, one blocker may be effective in handling the spiker's hits.

Ready position to block. The blocker must position himself one foot or so from the net and in line with the anticipated flight of the ball.

The jump. The blocker must be ready to jump immediately after the spiker does, his height being at its maximum when the ball is contacted.

Good jumpers may be effective taking off 6-12 inches from the net, while shorter players may need to be farther back to utilize a forward step and greater arm swing to gain more height in the jump.

Contact with the ball. The fingers should be spread and rigid in order to cover as much space as possible and to force the ball down into the opponent's court. If the set to the spiker is close to the net, the blocker should *attack block,* as in Figures 6.1 and 6.2.

Blockers unable to *attack block* should *defense block* or raise hands straight up to form a **wall**. Different sets require different blocking techniques. When a spiker gets an especially good set and a jump higher than the blockers, a *soft block* should be used. The hands are tilted back to deflect the ball up into the air for a teammate to play. (With using the International Rules, 3 hits are allowed *after* the "touch" on the block.)

Two blockers. When two players are working together, teamwork is essential for effectiveness of the block. The end blocker decides where to position the block by watching the set and the spiker. The center

Figure 6.1

Attack block tips.
1. Reach across net and use forceful wrist snap to put ball down to floor.
2. Pike body with legs also kicking under net to aid in power and balance.
3. After the block, straighten body quickly and bring legs, arms, and hands back away from the net.

Figure 6.2

Defense hit tips.
1. Jump and extend arms and hands in vertical plane or just **slightly** forward.
2. Be sure ball can't get between your hands or arms and the net.

Soft block tips.
1. *Jump with arms vertical, hands tilting back.*
2. Watch ball carefully to "get a piece of it."

blocker moves quickly to join the end blocker, plants the inside foot firmly so as not to collide with blocker, then both go up together for the block.

On two-player blocks, the end blocker uses slide steps to line up where the block is to be set up. The center blocker (See Figures 6.3 and 6.4) turns, steps, plants inside foot next to end blocker, and both go up together on the block.

Figure 6.3

Figure 6.4

Blockers must be careful to plant the inside foot before jumping to prevent drifting laterally, as the players in 6.5 are doing. This lack of control makes the block ineffective and is also likely to cause an injury upon landing.

Zone blocking. **Blocking the line and power angle shots.** The end blocker's hand nearest the sideline should be turned **in** to

Figure 6.5

contain the down-the-line spike. The center blocker's hands should stop the power-angle spike. (Figure 6.6.) There should be no more than 3-4 inches between blockers' hands.

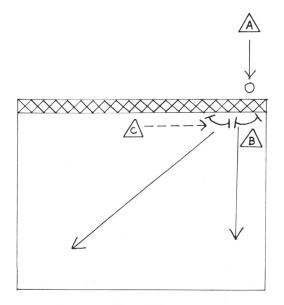

Figure 6.6

A. Spiker
B. End blocker
C. Center blocker

Power angle and cross-court spikes. Blockers should watch hitters carefully to determine their favorite sets and spikes. If a spiker never attempts a down-the-line spike, blockers would be more effective moving their block in and covering the power-angle and cross-court hits. (Figure 6.7.)

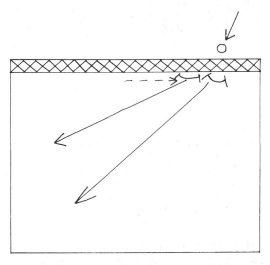

Figure 6.7

The **split block** may be used effectively against the spiker who always aims for the edges of a block and fails to see a hole in the center. See Figure 6.8. It is also an excellent

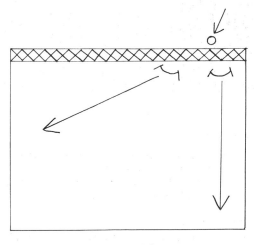

Figure 6.8

tactic use against the spiker who commits himself to the sharp cross-court shot, and when the center blocker is late in reaching his position following a wide shoot set to the sideline.

Figure 6.9 shows the spike finding the hole in the split block, in spite of good lateral *arm* movements by player 59 to stop the hit.

Figure 6.9

Additional blocking points.

1. On sets several feet off the net, the blocker's jump must be delayed to allow the extra time for the ball to reach the net.
2. On quick center hits, the center blocker should go up with the spiker. If the set is close to the net, an attack block should be used.
3. When the spike gets past the block, blockers should turn quickly and move off the net to be ready for the next play.
4. Blockers should refrain from reaching back to help out, as this usually results in tipping the ball away from the covering player.

5. Blockers should call out the "dink" to alert teammates of the play.
6. Blockers should learn to pull their hands down quickly and call "No" on hits that appear to be going out of bounds.
7. Center blocker must be agile and fast enough to move quickly along the net. If slow, he should be the end blocker in front of opponents' best spiker.

Warm-ups for blocking.

1. Players lined up along the wall. On signal, they slide one step to the right, jump and touch as high as possible with both hands, then land in controlled position. Repeat going left.
2. Players again lined up facing the wall. On signal, slide, jump and touch the wall, turn and are ready for a play.
3. Repeat above doing steps, plant and jump of center blocker.
4. Practice blocking from stool or low table at the net. Move hands only (laterally) to stop line and power angle spikes.
5. Lower net and have blockers work on attack blocks, then raise it to proper level and check progress.

Drill 1

Squad lines up along net, 3 on each side with partners of similar height. On signal, players slide one step, jump and attack block over net, then repeat in opposite direction.

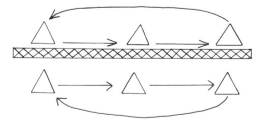

Figure 6.10

Footwork of center blocker can also use this formation.

Drill 2

Single blocker drill. Player A passes to D and moves to net for D's set. A spikes, B blocks, C, E, and F try to pick up the spike. Men rotate to spiking and blocking positions. Women rotate to setting and receiving positions.

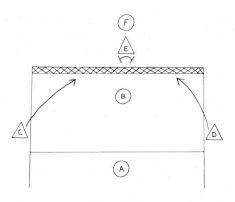

Figure 6.12

Drill 4

Two-blocker drill, with emphasis on center blocker moving to the block as setter **sets** ball.

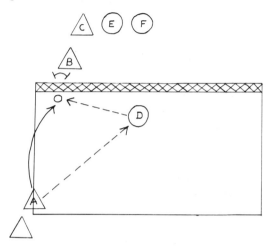

Figure 6.11

Drill 3

Center blocker drill. Player A passes to B who may either front set or back set, and blocker, E, must adapt to the play.

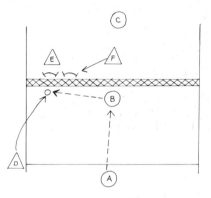

Figure 6.13

Student Evaluation of *Goof* List for Blocking

	Often	Sometimes	Seldom
1. Do I **drift** on my block due to failure to plant inside foot?			
2. Do I one-hand block, thereby giving up 50 percent of my blocking area?			
3. Do I forget to go **up** on close plays at the net to attack block?			
4. Do I block blindly, not seeing dinks and half-speed spikes?			
5. Do I jump too late for an effective block?			
6. Do I go up to block on free balls and no block situations?			
7. Do I fail to use the proper technique for the height I could jump?			
8. Do I forget to call "no" on spikes that are going out-of-bounds?			
9. Have I failed to master the technique of jumping **up** rather than forward?			
10. Do I forget to move off the net quickly and turn around for the next play when the spike goes through the block?			

Chapter 7

DIGS AND OTHER SAVES

Two-hand dig and half-roll. To practice receiving a hard, low ball, player should assume a deep squat position on the edge of a mat. A hard throw or spike is given to him that must be "cushioned" and directed back to leader. The weight is low over the back foot, and the player sits into a back half-roll as he completes the pass. See Figure 7.1.

Figure 7.1

To recover quickly to his feet, the player whips head, shoulders, arms and forward leg in a forward and upward motion. See Figure 7.2. Once player has confidence in this skill, he is ready to attempt more difficult saves.

Figure 7.2

Lateral dig and side roll. Player in Figure 7.3 is making a one-hand dig to his right, finishing with a side half-roll. See Figure 7.4.

Figure 7.3

Figure 7.4

To make this low play to his right, the player shifts his weight to his right leg, keeping the left leg and arm out for balance in other direction. He then contacts the ball with a cupped hand hit, the arm swinging across the body and rotating it for the sit to the thigh, buttocks and small of back, finishing as a back roll. Because of the speed of execution, the contact on the fall is taken mainly with the buttocks and back.

Overhand set of a low pass. Whenever player is able to get under the ball for a set, that is the play to make, as player in Figure 7.5 is demonstrating. However, on occasions when the ball approaches too fast and hard for a player to handle "cleanly," another technique may be in order.

Figure 7.5

The overhand dig. See Figure 7.6. To accomplish this technique, player cups hands and clasps them above the face, thumbs toward the face. The ball is contactsd by the outside edges of the hands, and rebounded upward. Caution: Players should not use this skill in place of plays that could be made with the overhand pass! Players who use this skill constantly are usually guilty of "lazy feet" and of playing out of position. It is a "save" that may only occur once or twice by a team during an entire match.

Figure 7.6

Digging Drill

Leader, A, stands on chair and spikes ball to B, who passes to C, who may set either D or E. Players rotate to each position and also take turns retrieving.

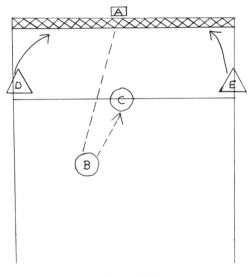

Figure 7.7

Chapter 8
TEAM TACTICS

Team tactics involve both the offensive and defensive play patterns or systems. As the first play of the game involves the receiving of the serve, that will be the first tactic covered.

Serve reception. 4-2 Offense. The most frequently used offense in volleyball is the 4-2 system, which consists of 4 spikers and two 2 setters. When the coed line-up involves 2 men and a woman in the front row, they are essentially employing the 4-2, with the C.F. as the setter and the L.F. and R.F. as the spikers. (Figure 8.1.)

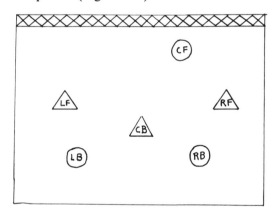

Figure 8.1

This "W" formation is ready made for the three player attack:
1. Forearm pass to the CF.
2. A set to the LF or RF.
3. A spike to win the rally.

Upon rotation, there are now two women and one man in the front row. Note the advantages and disadvantages of the receiving formation shown in 8.2.

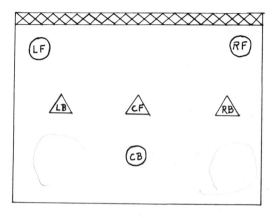

Figure 8.2

Advantage: The pass may be directed to either the LF or RF.

Disadvantages: There are only 4 players receiving the serve, and there are big "holes" behind the LB and RB players.

Switching. To improve upon the disadvantages described in Figure 8.2, the technique of switching positions should be introduced and practiced as soon as players seem to be ready. Players should be cautioned to maintain their original positions until it is known who will be handling the pass. Moving too quickly will alert opponents to serve **to** the switching players, causing a misplay. See Figure 8.3 for the switch of the C.F. to his more powerful spiking position.

Covering the spiker. Figure 8.4 shows a team practicing correct cover behind their spiker. Players must never allow themselves to be spectators in their game, but always moving to a more effective area of the court

43

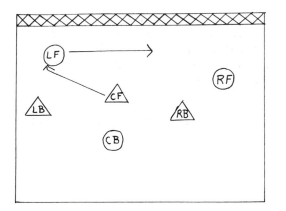

Figure 8.3

Figure 8.4

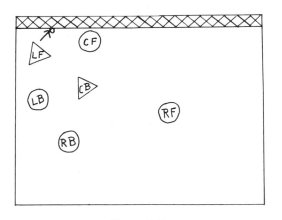

Figure 8.5

as each play develops. Figure 8.5 shows correct cover behind the L.F. spiker.

Defense against the spike. Many defenses have been devised for each offensive play. Every team needs to pick or create a defense that will best fit their strengths and nullify their opponent's attack. Two blockers should always be used in each blocking play, and every other defensive player should know his assignment and **be** there to do it. Figure 8.6 shows the block **taking the line and power shots** away from the spiker.

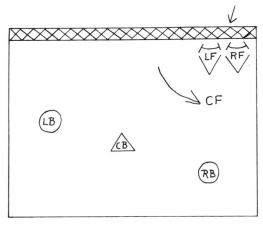

Figure 8.6

This block leaves the spiker with the more difficult cross-court shot.

In blocking the off-hand spike, Figure 8.7 shows the block giving the line but defending against the power angle and cross court spikes.

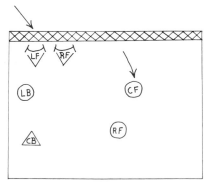

Figure 8.7

44

Upon rotation, with only one man in the front row, **coed rules allow a back row man to come to the front row to assist in blocking.** (Not in spiking.) Figure 8.8 shows the L.B. assisting in the block.

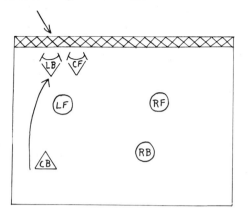

Figure 8.8

To block opponents' on hand spike when there is only one man in the front row, the L.B. moves to the net and the R.B. switches to defend against the power angle spike. Figure 8.9.

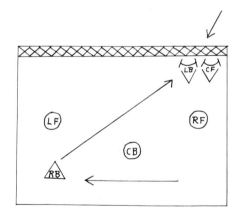

Figure 8.9

When the ball must be played back to opponents with a forearm pass, or any play other than a spike, "free ball" is called by the defense and they assume positions off the net as in Figure 8.10.

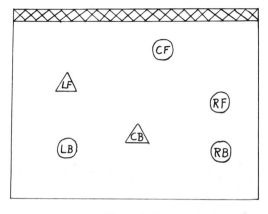

Figure 8.10

When a set is good enough for the spiker to hit in a downward angle, but not good enough to block, "no block" is called by the defense and they take covering positions as in Figure 8.11.

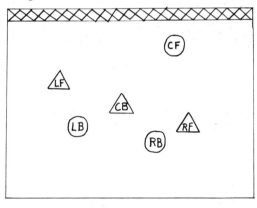

Figure 8.11

45

Figure 8.12 shows blockers taking away the power-angle and cross-court shots, so spiker hits down-the-line. Notice good cover position of player who is ready to dig the spike.

Figure 8.12

Terminology and Index
(Includes Page Numbers of Major Reference)

Above-the face. See *overhand set* or *pass*.

Ace. Serve that opponents are unable to receive; results in an outright point. p. 26

Antennae. Poles attached to the net directly above the sidelines to indicate balls legally in play.

Approach. Steps or path taken by spiker in moving to the ball. p. 29

Attack. The offense, or a team's efforts to hit the ball in such a manner as to score a point or gain the serve. p. 2

Attack block. See *block*.

Back-court. Area between 10 foot line and the endline.

Back-court spike. Offensive hit (spike) made by back-court player from the back-court area.

Back-court or back-row player. The right back, center back or left back player. pp. 1, 3

Back-set or reverse set, backward set-pass, flip-flop set. An overhand set in backward direction to spiker **behind** setter. pp. 5, 6, 7

Block. An attempt by one or more players to intercept a hard hit by opponents.
  a. Attack block, hard block or offensive block. Hands and arms are extended over net to keep ball on opponent's side.
  b. Defense block. Arms are straight up forming a **wall.**
  c. Soft block. Hands turned slightly up to deflect ball to back-court. pp. 35, 36

Bounce pass. See *forearm pass*.

Bump. See *forearm pass*.

Catch or lift. A foul in which ball is allowed to come to rest momentarily on any part of the body, usually the hands.

Centerline. The two inch line down the center of the court and directly under the net. pp. 1, 3

Change of courts. Teams change ends of court after each game and in the middle of the deciding game of a match.

Change of pace. See *spike*.

Court. 30′ × 60′ area for the game of volleyball. p. 1

Court coverage. The assigned positions for each player on offensive and defensive plays. pp. 43, 44, 45, 46

Cover. See *court coverage*.

Cross-court shot. See *spike*.

Cut shot. See *spike*.

Dead ball. Any ball not in play due to point, side-out, or suspension of play called by the referee.

Defense. The team not possessing the ball, or strategy by a team attempting to gain possession of the ball.

Defense block. See *block*.

Dig. Defensive play on a low ball, one or two hands may be used. Ball is contacted by the forearms whenever possible, but a fist or top of hand may be used for almost out-of-reach balls. p. 41

Dink. A faked spike which is tapped softly over the hands of the blockers. Wrist is kept stiff throughout the play. p. 31

Dive. Defensive move by player in playing a ball dropping in front, and then cushioning the landing with arms, chest and abdomen. For advanced players only!

Double hit. A foul, two hits by the same player when attempting to play the ball.

Down ball or down block. Blockers stay down and do not attempt to block when opponent's set is one that forces a weak return.

Down-the-line shot. See *spike.*

Drifting. Lateral movement of blockers while in the air, producing poor body control.

Drills. Specific practice techniques used to develop skills and to "warm-up" players for games.

Endlines. Backlines of the court.

Floater. See *serve.*

Floor positions. See *serving order positions.*

Foot fault.
    a. Foul committed by server stepping on or over the endline before contacting the serve.
    b. Player landing **beyond** the centerline before ball is dead.

Forearm pass, or bump, bounce, scoop. An underhand pass made by rebounding the ball off the forearms. Used for receiving serves and playing balls dropping below waist level. p. 15

Foul. Violation of the rules which results in **point** or **side-out.** pp. 2, 3

Free ball. An easy return of ball by opponents when no spike is expected, or an easy toss or pass to a team to start a practice rally. pp. 13, 45

Front-court or front-row player. The left forward, center forward or right forward player. p. 1

Front set. Overhand set made in direction setter is facing.

Game.
    a. A contest which ends when a team has scored 15 points and leads opponents by 2 or more points.
    b. If time is limited, a game may be determined by the team leading by 2 points after 8 minutes of play. In both a. and b., if a tie or 1 point lead exists at end of regular play, teams continue playing until a 2 point advantage occurs. p. 2

Good ball.
    a. Ball that lands on or inside the court lines.
    b. Ball passing over the net **inside** the antennae, which are placed directly above the sidelines.

Half-roll. Technique used to recover balance after a player digs a low ball. p. 41

Half-speed shot or hit. See *spike.*

Hit. Contact of the ball. Sometimes used for describing the spike.

Hitter. Spiker.

Inside the block.
    a. An attack play that forces the ball between the block and net.
    b. A sharp angle spike that evades the block.

International Volleyball Federation. Organization with headquarters in Paris, is responsible for all international volleyball competition and rules. pp. 1, 3

Inverted bump. See *overhand dig.*

Jap-set. See *play sets.*

Jump set. Set by player who has jumped into the air to make the play.

Jungle ball. A type of play with little control or attention to rules and strategy.

Kill. Sharply hit ball that opponents cannot return.

Lateral set. The shoulders of the setter are parallel to the direction of the set. For advanced players only!

Legal play. A play which does not result in a foul. (Some plays are legal, but **poor choices** as to strategy.)

Match. The best 2 out of 3 or 3 out of 5 games. p. 2

Multiple offense. All 3 front-row players are expected to spike and the ball is set by a back-row player.

National Association for Girls and Women in Sport. Organization designed to serve the needs of teachers, leaders and players in a variety of sports programs for girls and women. p. 1

Net.
 a. A cord, mesh divider directly above the centerline. It measures 32 ′ × 36 ″. p. 1
 b. Term used to describe served ball touching the net. p. 2
 c. Term describing a front-row player touching the net. p. 3

Net recovery. See *saves*.

No block. Blockers move off net when set is weak and no spike is expected. p. 45

Normal or regular set. High set toward sideline. p. 5

Off-hand or weak side. Hitting position where the ball must cross spiker's body to be in position to hit. (The right forward position for right-handed spikers.) p. 44

Offense.
 a. The team possessing the ball, the **attack.**
 b. Strategy or tactics used when possessing the ball.

Off-speed hit. See *spike*.

On-hand or strong side. Hitting position where spiker's hitting arm is on the same side as the approaching set. (The left forward position for right-handed spikers.) p. 45

One-set. See *play sets*.

Overhand dig. To play a hard spike at player's head, cup hands and clasp them together in position for the play, thumbs toward the face. Ball is contacted with the outside edges of the hands. p. 42

Overhand pass or set. The ball is played in front of the face using fingers of hands equally to direct a controlled pass or set. pp. 5, 6, 7, 8

Overhead volley. See *overhand pass or set*.

Overlap. Illegal position of a player when the ball is served. (Players should check placement of their **feet** in relation to player(s) on either side and in front or behind them.) p. 2

Overset. A set unintentionally set over the net to opponents' side.

Pass.
 a. Reception of the serve, first contact by the offense. p. 15
 b. Controlled movement of the ball between teammates. p. 5
 c. A free ball sent to opponents when no attack is possible. p. 13

Penetration. The act of blocking over the net on opponents' side. p. 36

Play sets. Planned set variations that are called out by the spiker.
 a. One-set or Jap-set; low, vertical set 6-12 inches above net.
 b. Two-set; low, vertical set 2-3 feet above net.
 c. Three-set. Ball is set at normal height between the center forward and end positions.
 d. Four-set or shoot-set. Ball is set low and fast to either sideline. p. 7

Point. Award given to the serving team when opponents commit a foul. p. 2

Power angle. See *spike*.

Power volleyball. Playing the game with greater stress on skill, strategy and force than is common in the former style of volleyball. p. 2

Punch serve. See *serve*.

Quick offense. Attack based on quickness in hitting rather than in power and full arm-swings. pp. 7, 31, 32

Quickie. One-set, Jap-set or low, quick, vertical sets. pp. 7, 31

Rally, volley. Play of the ball from time of service until the ball is dead.

Ready position. A player's position of body and feet in preparation for a particular technique. pp. 5, 6, 15

Receive. Maneuver used by player in handling the serve.

Referee. Main official of the game, is positioned on a stand at one end of the court.

Regular set. See *normal set.*

Roll. Technique used to recover balance after sideward move to save almost out-of-reach ball. p. 41

Rotation. Clockwise movement of players upon receiving the ball for the serve. p. 1

Roundhouse. See *serve.*

Save. Making a good play of a ball well beyond the normal range of coverage.
- a. Recovery of a ball hit into the net. p. 16
- b. "Punching" a high pass over net, deep into opponents' court. p. 8
- c. Digging a low ball almost out-of-reach. p. 41

Scoop. See *forearm pass.*

Screen. An attempt to illegally conceal a teammate's serve by several players lining up so as to obstruct an opponent's view of the serve.

Screw under. Technique used by player making low set or pass; finishing with pivoting motion and partial roll.

Serve. Technique used to put the ball in play to start the game, after each point, and after side-out. Some popular serves: underhand serve, sidearm serve, overhand floater (or punch), topspin and roundhouse. pp. 2, 23, 24, 25, 26

Serving order. The order in which players serve:
- 1. right back; 2. right forward; 3. center forward; 4. left forward; 5. left back; and 6. center back. These are also the floor positions for receiving the serve. p. 1

Set, set-up or set-pass. A precise pass play used to get the ball up near the net at a height advantageous for the spiker to hit the ball sharply downward into opponents' court. p. 5

Setter, set-passer or tosser. The player who sets the ball up for the spiker to hit.

Shoot-set. See *play sets.*

Shot. Spike.

Side-out. Term used to describe serving team's failure to score a point, the ball then going to opponents. p. 2

Soft block. See *block.*

Soft spike. See *spike.*

Spike. A hard hit made by a player who jumps into the air and forcefully drives the ball into the opponents' court down-the-line, cross-court, or to the area between for the power angle spike. pp. 29, 30, 37, 44, 45, 46

By taking speed and force away from the normal spike, the spiker can more carefully place the spike to "holes" in the court. These spikes are referred to as change-of-pace, half-speed or soft spikes. A soft spike deliberately deflected off the blocker's hands is called a wipe off shot.

A cut or turn shot is one made at an acute angle with arm and hand swinging away from spiker's body. p. 31

Spiking line. Line 10 feet from net. Back-row players may not spike from in front of this line. pp. 1, 3

Spiker or hitter. Attack player who drives the ball sharply downward into opponents' court.

Switch. An interchange of positions on the court for better offensive and defensive play. pp. 43, 44, 45

Systems of attack or offensive systems. The strategy or tactics employed for best use of a team's spikers and setters:
- a. 4-2, four spikers and two setters. In coed play, with two men and one woman in the front row, this system is used. p. 43

b. 3-3, three spikers and three setters. In coed play, with one man and two women in the front row, this system would be used.

Tactics. Offensive and defensive procedures used by teams to control the ball. p. 43

Throw. A ball not "cleanly" hit.

Topspin. Forward spin imparted to the ball by snapping wrist vigorously at contact.

Trajectory. Flight or path of the ball.

United States Volleyball Association. Association composed of organizations; sponsors major volleyball activities and represents volleyball on the United States Olympic Committee. p. 1

Verbal tips or cues. Calls made by a player to teammates to ensure the proper play. (Mine, out, girl, free ball, no block, etc.) p. 20

Volley. See *rally*.

Bibliography and Selected References

Bertucci, Bob, "Chalk Talk," *Volleyball Magazine,* February, 1977, p. 20-23, Volleyball Inc., 812 Anacapa Street, Santa Barbara, California, 93101.

Coleman, James E., and Liskevych, Taras, N., *Pictorial Analysis of Power Volleyball,* Creative Sports Books, P.O. Box 2244, Hollywood, California, 90028, 1974.

Egstrom, Glen H., and Schaafsma, Frances, *Volleyball,* second edition, Wm. C. Brown Company Publishers, Dubuque, Iowa, 52001, 1972.

Long, Ron, "On Two-Man Beach Volleyball," *Volleyball Magazine,* Summer, 1976, p. 59-64, Volleyball Inc., 812 Anacapa Street, Santa Barbara, California, 93101.

McGown, Carl, *It's Power Volleyball* Committee on Studies and Development, United States, Volleyball Association, Pacific Palisades, California, 90272, 1968.

McReavy, Marilyn, "The Soft Set," *Division For Girls and Women's Sports,* 1973-75, p. 29-31, AAHPER, 1201 Sixteenth Street, N.W., Washington, D.C., 20036.

National Association for Girls and Women In Sport, *Volleyball Guide,* AAHPER, 1201 Sixteenth Street, N.W., Washington, D.C., 20036, Publishsd Every Two Years, Formerly Known as Division For Girls and Women's Sports.

Scates, Allen E., and Ward, Jane, *Volleyball,* Allyn and Bacon, Boston, Massachusetts, 01867, 1969.

Schaafsma, Frances, and Heck, Ann, *Volleyball For Coaches and Teachers,* Wm. C. Brown Company Publishers, Dubuque, Iowa 52001, 1971.

Shay, C., (Consultant) *Volleyball Skills Tests Manual,* AAHPER, 1201 Sixteenth Street, N.W., Washington, D.C., 20036.

Slaymaker, Thomas, and Brown, Virginia H., *Power Volleyball,* Revised Edition, W. B. Saunders Co., Philadelphia, Pa., 19105, 1975.

Stokes, Roberta, "Power Volleyball Drills," *Coaching: Women's Athletics,* March/April, 1977, p. 44, 45, 51, P.O. Box 867, Wallingford, Connecticut, 06492.

Thigpen, Janet, *Powsr Volleyball For Girls and Women,* Second Edition, Wm. C. Brown Company Publishers, Dubuque, Iowa, 52001, 1974.

Tom, Marilyn, Luckman, Margaret A., *Coed Volleyball,* The National Press, Palo Alto, California, 94304, 1966.

Vannier, Maryhelen, Ed. D., and Poindexter, Ed. D., *Individual and Team Sports for Girls and Women,* W. B. Saunders Co., Philadelphia, Pa., 19105, p. 667-718.

Veronee, Marvin, Editor, *United States Volleyball Association Official Rules,* Guyes Printing Company, 615 North Stanton Street, El Paso, Texas, 79901.

Wyckoff, Irene, "React, Receive, Respond," *NAGWS Volleyball Guide,* AAHPER, 1201 Sixteenth Street, N.W., Washington, D.C., 20036, p. 21-23, 1975-1977.